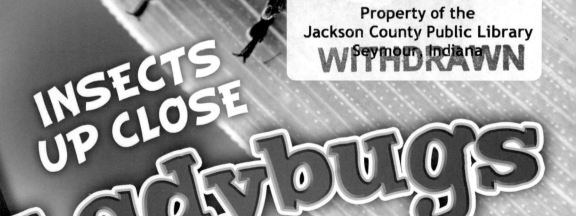

INSECTS UP CLOSE

Ladybugs

by Christina Leaf

BLASTOFF! READERS

BELLWETHER MEDIA • MINNEAPOLIS, MN

Note to Librarians, Teachers, and Parents:

Blastoff! Readers are carefully developed by literacy experts and combine standards-based content with developmentally appropriate text.

Level 1 provides the most support through repetition of high-frequency words, light text, predictable sentence patterns, and strong visual support.

Level 2 offers early readers a bit more challenge through varied simple sentences, increased text load, and less repetition of high-frequency words.

Level 3 advances early-fluent readers toward fluency through increased text and concept load, less reliance on visuals, longer sentences, and more literary language.

Level 4 builds reading stamina by providing more text per page, increased use of punctuation, greater variation in sentence patterns, and increasingly challenging vocabulary.

Level 5 encourages children to move from "learning to read" to "reading to learn" by providing even more text, varied writing styles, and less familiar topics.

Whichever book is right for your reader, Blastoff! Readers are the perfect books to build confidence and encourage a love of reading that will last a lifetime!

This edition first published in 2018 by Bellwether Media, Inc.

No part of this publication may be reproduced in whole or in part without written permission of the publisher. For information regarding permission, write to Bellwether Media, Inc., Attention: Permissions Department, 5357 Penn Avenue South, Minneapolis, MN 55419.

Library of Congress Cataloging-in-Publication Data

Names: Leaf, Christina.
Title: Ladybugs / by Christina Leaf.
Description: Minneapolis, MN : Bellwether Media, Inc., 2018. | Series: Blastoff! Readers. Insects Up Close | Audience: Age 5-8. | Audience: K to grade 3. | Includes bibliographical references and index.
Identifiers: LCCN 2016052749 (print) | LCCN 2016053547 (ebook) | ISBN 9781626176676 (hardcover : alk. paper) | ISBN 9781681033976 (ebook)
Subjects: LCSH: Ladybugs–Juvenile literature.
Classification: LCC QL596.C65 L43 2018 (print) | LCC QL596.C65 (ebook) | DDC 595.76/9–dc23
LC record available at https://lccn.loc.gov/2016052749

Editor: Christina Leighton   Designer: Maggie Rosier

Printed in the United States of America, North Mankato, MN.

Table of Contents

What Are Ladybugs?

Ladybugs are colorful **beetles**. Their polka-dot bodies stand out!

Red, orange, or yellow covers hide ladybug wings. The covers are hard and rounded.

covers

wing

Ladybug legs are short. A ladybug also has two small **antennae** on its head.

ACTUAL SIZE: seven-spotted ladybug

antennae

Ladybug Life

Ladybugs make their homes in grasslands, forests, and gardens.

Ladybugs help farmers. They munch on pests like **aphids**.

aphid

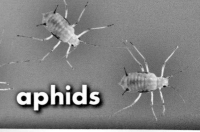

FAVORITE FOOD:

aphids

In winter, ladybugs **hibernate** in big groups. They come out again in spring.

hibernating
ladybugs

15

Growing Up

A female ladybug lays hundreds of eggs. **Larvae** break out after a few days.

**female
ladybug**

eggs

larva

A larva attaches itself to a plant when it is big. It becomes a **pupa**.

pupa

LADYBUG
LIFE SPAN:
2 to 3 years

Then, the insect changes again. The pupa becomes an adult ladybug!

adult ladybug

Glossary

antennae
feelers connected to the head that sense information around them

hibernate
to pass the winter by sleeping or resting

aphids
small insects that harm plants by sucking the juice from them

larvae
baby insects that have come from eggs; larvae often look like worms.

beetles
insects with hard outer wings that cover inner flying wings

pupa
a young insect that is about to become an adult

To Learn More

AT THE LIBRARY

Carr, Aaron. *Ladybugs.* New York, N.Y.:
AV2 by Weigl, 2016.

Guillain, Charlotte. *Life Story of a Ladybug.*
Chicago, Ill.: Heinemann Library, 2015.

Mattern, Joanne. *It's a Good Thing There
Are Ladybugs.* New York, N.Y.: Children's
Press, 2015.

ON THE WEB

Learning more about
ladybugs is as easy
as 1, 2, 3.

1. Go to www.factsurfer.com.

2. Enter "ladybugs" into the search box.

3. Click the "Surf" button and you will see a
   list of related web sites.

With factsurfer.com, finding more information
is just a click away.

Index

The images in this book are reproduced through the courtesy of: Yellowj, front cover; Christian Musat, pp. 4-5; InsectWorld, pp. 6-7, 8-9; Eric Gevaert, pp. 10-11; Jolanda Aalbers, pp. 12-13; Kletr, p. 13; Lamzinvnikola, pp. 14-15; lior2, pp. 16-17; nounours, p. 17; Eduardo Estellez, pp. 18-19; irin-k, pp. 20-21; ninii, p. 22 (top left); Radu Bercan, p. 22 (center left); syaochka, p. 22 (bottom left); Philip Bird LRPS CPAGB, p. 22 (top right); chinahbzyg, p. 22 (center right); AC Rider, p. 22 (bottom right).